NATIONAL GEOGRAPHIC

A Good Place for a City

Stevie Prince

Many cities are located near
bodies of water.
Some cities are near rivers.
Some cities are near lakes.
Other cities are near oceans.

Being near water is a good
place for a city.
Ships can carry goods to and from
a city near water.

New York

New York is located on the Hudson River near the Atlantic Ocean. Ships from other countries bring goods into New York harbor. Then trucks carry the goods to other parts of the country.

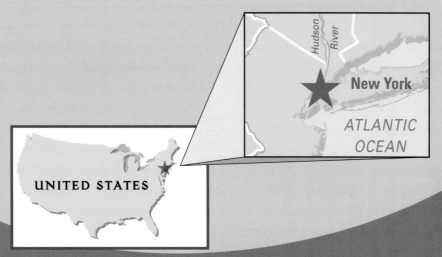

UNITED STATES

Hudson River

New York

ATLANTIC OCEAN

Pittsburgh

Pittsburgh is located where two rivers join together to form the Ohio River. Pittsburgh is known for its industry. Coal and steel are shipped on barges down the Ohio River.

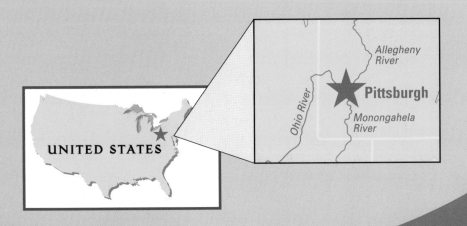

Chicago

10

Chicago is located on Lake Michigan.
Lake Michigan is one of the
Great Lakes.
Food grown on farms in the Midwest
comes to Chicago by train.
Then the food is shipped to other places.

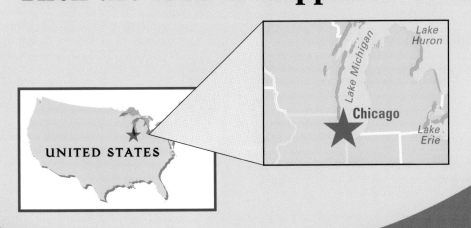

Los Angeles

12

Los Angeles is located on the Pacific Ocean.

It is the busiest port in the country. Ships bring goods from other countries into this port.

Ships carry goods from the United States to other countries, too.

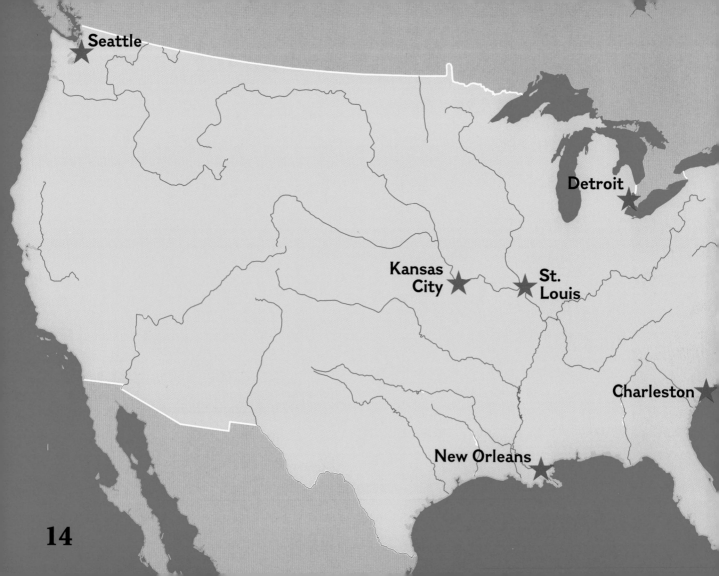

Seattle

Detroit

Kansas City

St. Louis

Charleston

New Orleans

These cities are located near water, too.
Being near water is a good place
for a city.

Index